THOUGHTS FROM THE OAK

THOUGHTS FROM THE OAK

AUDREY COLASANTI POETRY

THE **BLACK SPRING**
PRESS GROUP

First published in 2023
by The Black Spring Press Group
Maida Vale Publishing imprint
Grantully Road, Maida Vale, London W9,
United Kingdom

Typeset with graphic design by Edwin Smet

978-1-913606-60-2

*The editor has generally followed American spelling and punctuation
at the author's request.*

BLACKSPRINGPRESSGROUP.COM

TABLE OF CONTENTS

iii.

butternut

my first son was born
yellow

the underripe yellow
of an autumn squash

pulled too soon
from the farmer's field

I loved him instantly
& absolute

my sweetsick
yellow brave

not knowing how true
the brave part

in the hurricane years
ahead

I   his mother
squash blossom

bearer
of unusual fruit.

not periwinkle

my second son was born blue
a charcoal ashy blue
let's call it chimney sweep blue

born the color of a chimney
sweep's cheeks
he was raced away from me

in a slick white ambulance
flashing cherry red lights

two minutes prior
he had been curled
in my womb

the tender hat
of my belly button
snug atop his head

two minutes forward
& he was gone
on to the dark grey forest

of infants in incubators
scalpels & stitches

gone
before I could even
spit out my placenta

a slimy black boot
laced with veins
& soot.

in my arms – thoughts from the oak

what does the blue jay think
when an egg falls from its nest?
how does the spider handle the bat
feasting on its young?
each time another leaf slips from my limbs
it hurts all the way down to my heartwood
I feel the emptiness in my arms
the immutable echo of vacant boughs
my roots untethered

I once saw a fawn
dangling from the power line
beneath my crown
eagle
owl
I do not know who dropped it there

as I looked into the black
marble eyes of the fawn
struck open
tongue lolling
neck snap folded over the line
I worried
where is its mother?
will she think to look up
to find her missing child?
will she feel the gnawing pain
in her heartwood?
the razor-sharp arrow
shredding the bark of her soul?

I do not know how a bullfrog croaks
I do not know what the mole thinks
blind above ground
but the stabs of motherhood?
well
the harsh season
the brutal rake
the bonfire
hand me a seed
& I can tell you
sorrow awaits.

I

yellow

my house here is painted
the yellow color of fresh butter
an enormous yellow lantern
sheds its light on the terrace
this avenue entirely yellow
decked with buttercups
– a yellow sea
how lovely yellow is!

there is no blue without yellow
if you do blue
than do yellow
surely
yellow ochre
yellow lettuces
yellow white pear trees
a field of yellow wheat
the strange silhouette of a drawbridge
against a huge yellow sun

certain stars are lemon yellow
the lighted square
greenish citron yellow
the chrome yellow sky
against yellow earth
harsh & broken
in which yellows will burst
high up   the yellow
turns to pink
turns to green

oh   what a fellow
yellow.

the mink-headed guest – thoughts from the oak

he is a curious one, this child hiding
in the fork of my branch, dangling his sneakers
over the edge, peering at the world below
as if an interloper into the wrong

religion. I try to soothe him with the laughter
in my leaves, the calming rivers that furrow
my bark. he delights in the little gifts I have
hidden up high. feathers. acorns. the fuzzy

caterpillar that will curl in his palm, asleep
he is a curious one, yes, but hugged tight
in the crook of my arms, his loneliness
is less. becalmed, at its most. I like this

child. he is not like some others, born boring
too perfect. he would never harm me, nor call
me insignificant. his back to my belly
it warms me.

counting all the cracks in the sidewalk

count how many times
you have driven around the lake
your car on an endless merry-go-round
round & round you go
past the logs the turtles sun on
past the rose garden
the beach
count all the turtles
seven
count the logs
three
count how long it takes
the girl in the bikini to stub
out her cigarette in the waves
how quick the ember dies
sizzles to nothing
count the thud of your tires
count the thud of your heartbeat
count how many times
your sweetsickchild kicks at the car door
screaming *I wish I were dead I wish I were dead*
twenty five   twenty six   thirty eight   forty nine
count how long it takes
for the window glass to feel the boot heel
& shatter all over the backseat
count your breaths
count all the fractures
in your fairy-tale life
count each lap around the lake
count dracula's
count chocula's

count basie & monte cristo
just keep driving
keep counting.

because he had visions

no lamps with cords
no pillowcases
no forks
shoelaces yanked out
fingernails clipped
no belts
no brushes
& no balloons

no   no   to the balloons

kids here   they pop the balloons
make nooses out of the string
stuff the latex down their throats
because breathing is no longer
a desirable thing

sponge bob & the little mermaid
whisked down the hall in the hands
of a tsk-ing nurse
scurried into an elevator
to the cancer ward instead

bobbing on their strings
red   orange   cotton candy pink
all pumped up in colorful clothes
cheeks abloat with jolly
funsters at the wrong parade.

weaning off paxil

love is a circle
of purple pearls
you will wear
forever

even after it fades
from its deep
purple seams
to blue green

to just an invisible
bite mark
where your child latched
on his teeth & screamed

wailed across his hospital room
shaking your wrist
back & forth
between his mouth

love   you have found
is a jaw searching
for something
to hold on to.

after doctor number five

said
it might be
schizophrenia
or just
bipolar
or maybe   even
mad king george disease
the monarch madness

after doctor number five
chuckled
& said
frankly   I just don't know
I fled
a crazed wild mother
thinking her moving legs
could erase everything behind her
as if life were a chalkboard
& her feet   the wet sponge

after doctor number five
my legs scrubbed with a fury
all the way into the parking lot
where they collapsed
buckled right into a puddle
of mud & grease

beneath my palms & knees
squirmed an oily dark mirror
filmed with coppers & greens

I had crumpled into a rainbow
being eaten by gasoline
my wail so savage
I snapped
a rib.

**doctor number six
(your child has epilepsy)**

joan of arc told of her flames
the visions   voices
blazing as she prayed

lewis carroll   he too
was cursed by the spinning
dark well

wrote of elixirs & sweets
that might change him
save him

the little vial
DRINK ME
the piece of cake
EAT ME

& vincent   dear vincent
he took to the fields
to paint it away

the trees
TOUCH ME
the flowers
SMELL ME

& all those paintings
of peasants
curl-backed over their spades

raking & raking at the fields
digging potatoes
digging up roots

digging up rocks
digging
& digging

the shovel
DIG WITH ME
we will find sunshine
under this stone.

seizures (plural plural)

the sour aromas that vex the nose
spectacular satellites that rocket
beneath flickerburst lids

you have been visited by staggering visions
with colors so rich & vigorous
they do not even exist
on a pantone color wheel

you tell us you have seen god
but not *that* god
& this moment is not
altogether unsettling

mouth bloodied
bruises beginning their catwalk
you do not know where
you are   or what

has just happened
why
your front tooth
is dangling from its socket

you cry for god
to kill you
but let me
drape my hand
across your forehead   first.

in the room

is a mattress on the floor
      less distance to fall
a bookshelf
with books about heroes
& superheroes
& super duper
far away lands

the word optimism
is scrawled in magic
marker on the windows
the walls
the door

the door
that is slammed
shut
a lot

but left open
when the eyelids begin
to flicker & roll
foot rapid tapping
its s.o.s.

the door
left open
says *listen*
for me

please.

roommates

i.
fairview riverside
kyle

my dad is coming today
he said he would come today
have you seen my dad
he promised he was coming
he said he would bring me some taco bell
after five days of the above lines
you leave your own son to go find a taco bell
you bring back a quesarito   crunch wrap supreme
& five bean burritos   one for every day
a son asked for his father   who never showed
but sure loves   his taco bell

ii.
cleveland clinic
deshawn

his mom brought homemade ribs & cornbread
sat on the side of his bed singing hymns
licking sauce off her thumbs
he just fakin'   i aint got no son with this thing
doctor full a' bullshit

iii.
mayo clinic
james

a limp rag doll   all soft stuffing and crooky sweet smile
seizure dropped right through a kitchen window
while watching a hawk dismember a rabbit out on the lawn

the breaking glass   little boy hurtling out
crunching to the patio   twitchquivering on the cement
it was too much   for the mighty hawk
he got full spooked
dropped the rabbit & fled

flew so high up into the clouds he just disappeared
left behind an entire meal of steaming guts
& bunny juice right there in the grass
some slaughters
even the fierce have trouble with it.

milk on the walls

orange juice
still in its glass

maple syrup
pancake attached

the hardboiled egg
it burst
a sulfur grenade

yellow yolk
brown shell

this   my friends
another dinner
in hell

we blame it
on the meds

lorazapam
diazepam
clonazepam
something
& something-a-pams

13 pills a day can do that
turn one's nerve cells
into a wailing picasso
dali throwing dishes

crazy twitches
bloodstream a gurgle
with poison witches

such a dilemma
this knife to the throat
cuff to the hands

without the lorazapam
diazepam
clonazepam
something
& something-a-pams
death lurks

jerks its blade
taunting us
with a too-early timeline

so we clean up
the artwork
weeping off the walls
saying not a word

dipping our rags
into the deep bucket
of hope & deals

palms blistered
from chlorine
& clawing.

hex

a voodoo doll & really sharp pins

the woman who called your son a freak
pin to the mouth

all those people who gawked at the writhing
but never stepped forward to help

pins to the eyes
pins to their cowardly feet

go ahead   it's okay
no one has to see

no one needs to know
you had to go back to the store

for more pins
& enjoyed the errand immensely.

for the mothers

you know who you are

you sleep with one ear cocked
to the bedroom door & down the hall
ever listening for the sandbag thump against plaster
the banging of bed boards, books falling off shelves
as if flung by fairies

you know who you are

you have attended the dented bicycle
the chipped teeth & bitten lips
the shattered rainbow
of your child's dreams

yes   you know who you are

counting out pills from bright orange bottles
wondering instead about nostrums & salves
you would give your child eye of newt
lung of jungle lizard
if you knew it would help

you would swallow lightning bolts
to save your child
from *this*

yes   you know who you are

a kite   holding its arms to the storm
here   take me.

only for soldiers

but…
but…
I…
& how was I…
it has been just so…
all the calls to…
ambulances blaring their…
blood all over the…
lips ripped in…
teeth shattered like…
against the side of a…
the edge of a…
one time   onto the hood of a…
brain swelled up like…
even in the seat of an…
as its wheels touched down at…
all those broken…
stitches to the…
stitches in the…
fifty
one hundred
one hundred fifty pounds of solid…
falling into my arms
body a concrete…
sizzling with…
& did i say
onto the hood of a…
flew right through the…
bicycle landed in a nearby tree.

II

blue

is strutting down the sidewalk in a tiny blue coat & toy store kepi
all six-year-old swagger & little boy brass   the gun in his hands
shoots rubber bands   droopy stringed bullets all over the grass

when he stumbles to his knees feigning wounds from a battle
blue cries out to his troops   *I've been hit! I've been hit!*
damn rebel got me in the butt!   potato grenades   swords of plastic
the others roll on the lawn   tittering   fantastic

me too! me too! my butt's bleeding too!   wriggling   giggling
they salute blue from chubby wrists   grass stained pants
sergeant! shall we retreat?   they squeal & chant
never! blue hollers   stumbling to standing
never! ever!   voice quavering   commanding

only cowards   you dummy d-d-d-ick dums   give in to defeat!
veins a-pop on his forehead   blue clutches his fists
indignant rocks on skinny sticks   when you are six
you know what you feel   but not how to say
I've been to death's gate   felt it blow on my ears
grab your bayonets   proud soldiers   there is hell to pay.

premonition – thoughts from the oak

the crows have been howling since sunrise
not the caw caw caw
that screeches from their lungs
while picking flesh from the dead
cat on the side of the road

or while plucking
unripe sprouts of corn from the failing stalk
no   the sound
startling this morning's sky
is the distinct call of sorrow

a cacophony of wretched keening
wails from a hundred yellow beaks
tortured   ululating
they yelp across the woods
a hundred aching pallbearers

their death chant deaf
to the fox who circles below
slinking copper around tree trunks
waiting for another fledgling
to stumble & fall from my nest.

four days old

because I still cannot peel the skin
off that fig   let me tell you   instead
of the other children nearby

bed to the left   a tiny blinking walnut
slash-space-age-appliance   wires   tubes
one winces for the nut-brown newborn beneath

bed to the right   a jenga of broken bones
face a smashed melon   two cops   three nurses
one mother   irked
I told you   she fell off a shopping cart

the father pops fries in his mouth
as if buttered popcorn at a movie show
nah, bitch, she fell off the couch

the bed   the edge of my knees
his story   a ledge of tectonic plates
shifting beneath an oily pink tongue

the induction is so fast   into this gehenna
ringed with flames   still pure babes
meant to play hercules with peewee hearts

toy-sized lungs   tongues   that have yet
to taste milk   mere hatchlings still wet
with egg-sac & wonder

when in hell   it is difficult
to believe in god & life's meaning

the lights are too bright   something keeps beeping

I need a soft sweater   I need someone
to hug me   but not   touch me.

stitches

in the hospital gift
shop they sell t-shirts
that say *chicks dig scars*
we try to tell you
this is true
& it is
they do

we also remind you
what a warrior you are
heart stopped
five
    times

ribcage sawed open
five
    times

sewn
back up again
five
    times

you were only
four
    days old
    the first
    time

the surgeon
a tender tailor

stitched you with catgut
polyester
one
   time
   stapled metal wire

you never make it
past the x-ray
at TSA
your chest such a zigzag
of mysterious thread.

grandma patsy becomes a priest

lord hear our prayer

baptized you at bedside
with shaking palms
the *our father*
recited in smattering latin

her nerves so wrought
she forgot
to sprinkle the holy water
collected from the bathroom tap

but she did perform
some sort of sign of the cross
with her thumb
to your temples

crumbled crackers
from her purse bottom
used as ashes

lord hear our prayer.

faith in the heart surgeon

with the smoker's shakes
fingers itching for another cig
the taste of marlboros seducing his lips

faith
that his delirium tremens ceases to be
as he works his scalpel
slicing deep

such pressure this   assigned to faith
that imperfect vapor
with its renowned disputes

faith
I wonder   did the woman who saved a monarch butterfly
its wing torn by a playful cat
feel this strain to her missionary

with tweezers   glue   & a spare wing from a fallen swallowtail
did she feel a judgment to her proud religion   her decision
to pray at the altar of broken wings

do the butterfly seamstress & the surgeon with the smoker's shakes
feel the same call   when   heads bent down   they touch
the soul of another   each cut & stitch
so close to the crucial vein

perhaps this is power   not faith
the day you are summoned to be savior-saint
as if you were god   gandhi   genghis khan

somewhere   a butterfly exists with an orange wing
on the left   blue wing sewn to the right

when the butterfly seamstress opened her palms
& watched her miracle alight   did she know

someone else   far away   was also
praying their knuckles skyward
bones on fire
under the too-hot sun?

balm or blitz

I.

the human heart is its own timepiece & electrical outlet
sparking with enough energy to produce 100,000 beats per day
even when removed from inside the chest the heart of a human
can continue beating   a stubborn Rolex refusing to die
or simply confused by what is happening

II.

you remember
the grouse that slammed into the windowpane
throwing its heart right out of its ribcage
a heart   once nestled inside
beating with ferocity

now on the outside
still & compliant
rolling to a dead stop
amongst the shattered glass

there was no electricity sparking out
in one last sputter of light
no dripping blood
shocking us with a violent stream

we expected something more
something epic at that moment of passage
a shriek or violent jerk, an explosion even
like a fireworks factory struck by lightning

ravaged in roaring flames

one of its legs did give a brief kick
& then that was it
as if brushing away its past
& all the moments behind
were not the dark hour

we fear it must be
but an eloquent release
a relief even —
stopped still
in its quiet triumph.

III.

my heart is a broken bone
masked as muscle & veins
it bleeds yellow & blue & green
the bloodshed of fear & sorrow

& a festering innocence
still startled when the archfiend arrives
pounding on my door, there to steal
the last breadcrumbs & my stoutest mead

my heart   it is a mary poppins coin
purse of endless trinkets inside
sea urchins swans hammers honeycomb
you will find flowering jasmine inside my heart

as well as fetid worms   sharp swords
& sugar cubes so sweet
they can   at times   rot teeth
with their cloying overabundance

there are children in there
clinging   with their nails
to the walls of my heart
it can hardly stand the pressure

pulsing with each beat
my heart   smaller than a coconut
just larger than a dinner roll
how does it hold all that it does

& not leak on occasion
the resin that drips from my heart
it could be edible   on the good days.

ransom

to whom it may concern:

we have your child   we will return him in exchange for your SPLEEN
BACKBONE & INTESTINAL FORTITUDE   please put said spleen
backbone & stomach juices in a titanium chest   bound in iron chains
so that said items will be difficult for you to recover in the future
once you have relinquished all holds on sanity   self-care   & maintaining
your household   you will find your child faring far better then you
through this kidnapping of laughter & sweet sleep   do not attempt
to contact the authorities as they will not understand the threat
to your family & heartache ensued

signed
yours in despair

illness

aromatherapy

there is the distinct tang
of antiseptic
& stale pajamas
& as you pass certain rooms
white lilies
that sad syrupy scent
reserved for hospitals
& funeral parlors
the fading
& faded
every meal
on its plastic blue tray
smelling
of canned corn
tinned peaches
the family waiting
lounge
thick with nicotine
fast fried chips
the undeniable notes
of inhaling
& gulping
sucking in
& swallowing
all that dread
it is everywhere
the perfume
of the living
& dying
& trying
the constant attar

of floor 7-b
jail
bastion
cauldron
zoo.

skedaddle

just flee! flee!
flee to the woods!
run to where the giant trees grow
hurdle logs
jump the stream
feel the burs & thorns
bite at your knees
crawl through the bramble
scramble up the last hill
run to where the wolves run
on padded feet
deep deep
just flee!
the deeper you go
the farther from here
as you scare up the quail
asleep in the weeds
listen to the beat
of his wings
there is panic in there
frenzied   in fright
addled skedaddled
by your boots unannounced
but watch him now
how nimble he falls
back into his forest
of zen
a sigh from his beak
cluck of the tongue
this moment now past
forgotten

he nestles
back into the bush

   becalmed

      heart stilled

         hush   hush…

ghost scars

how can we not have them?
you   me
your brother   your father

you cannot mend a ghost
at least   not completely
but one can try

this kind of stitching
takes a slow needle
begets an embroidery basket

filled with heavy floss
some days   we grab the ghost
& work on its fragile fabric

more often
the ghost walks the heartache
halls beneath our ribs

with trembling fingers
we jab   poke   jab
too shaken to stab

in the needle
& yank out the shadows
still lurking.

my warship

is a brickship with lilacs in the yard
it is no goodship lollipop
outfitted with bonbons & lemon drops

too often   she is a sorrowship
bruised & muddied
haunted by battles still fighting

she creaks & groans
pops bolts when the pressure
on her walls gets too tight

someone is always with fever
misery   a passel of ravenous fleas
there is a medicine chest

beds with good pillows
rum & gin   a set of mala beads
the shine prayed right out of them

my warship   it is a tatteredship
tippyship   a guttedship
hollow cheeked & weary

despair falls from our gums
in gory black stones   maybe
we just don't eat enough limes.

gram negative rods

it took a full week for his blood
to bloom   to fold out onto its
glass slide like a lotus blossom
in the mud   thirty-two blood draws

& seven days for his blood to
flower   pink rimmed with saffron
rimmed with fuchsia   a rare
tulip-crocus-rose   so miniscule

only the meticulous eye
of a microscope could attest
to its bud   we think it's the big
things that will get us   the loud

& dramatic car crash   people
lining the street to see the crunched
hood   broken glass   we deserve this
don't we? something momentous

epochal even   to usher
us out to the edge & if we
are lucky   back again for round
two   not a tiny freak floret

blossoming in the bloodstream
right above one's heart   setting its
roots   fanning its poison petals.

with a twist

shaken not stirred   because my hands
need to crush ice between the walls
of a martini shaker

at some point it all becomes a comedy
wake up one morning so sucked dry
husked out   a bruised strip of lemon
becomes breakfast

I taste the dry gin
guffaw   snort through my nose
wriggle my toes in their socks
wonder how they are doing
with all this.

girdling – thoughts from the oak

my dear
how can I break this to you gently?
the easiest way to destroy a beating heartwood
is to bring the demise on slowly

the most effective method
and I know this
from having observed it myself
is to hack a ring all the way around

the ribs of a once stout tree
hack & hack
until your blade is bloodied
and you sever the sugar source

causing a sucking anemia to the soul
if the heartwood is a strong one
it will try to jump the girdle
and heal itself

a stout dose of poison will deter
this pompous behavior
once the arteries have been slit
and venom sloshed into the open wound

it is impossible to keep standing upright
it may take time, but eventually
the heartwood will give way
with a thunderous crash

leaving the field empty
of yet another good shepherd.

III

bone vase

if you ask a mother how much she loves her children
you must be prepared for her to snap

off her kneecaps & stuff each cavity
with brutal flowers   iris   larkspur

lily of the valley   blooms   that if bitten into
could give you great discomfort

as you tiptoe around her kneecap garden
being mindful of the fragility of petals

as well as raw sinew & bone
you will notice that this mother is buckling

under the weight of her giant bouquet
just look how she folds herself into strange

contortions to caress all the flowers
exploding from her knees

but also notice   how in this posture
she can rest her chin on a profusion

of blooms & cup them to her squatted chest
a sumo wrestler inhaling

the scents of fresh dirt   play-doh
& sticky taffy

how much does a mother love her children
she will risk arthritis & nerve damage
curvature of the spine to show you
if you put your ear to her kneecap

garden   you might even hear the ocean
of a howling heart.

incantation for this day

oh iris   mother of rainbows
oh algea   she who scrubs away pain
dear gelos   god of laughter
and the wisdom of contentment

grant me the night vision of a bat
the patience of a seed
and a pinch of dirt that you have trod upon
for   your feet are my oars

help to line my skirts with buckshot
and thimbleberry thorns
guide me as I walk my day
swinging my sharpened skirts far & wide

oh fu-shen
branwen
oh   lucky rabbit's foot affixed to my keys
grant me the confidence to pulverize

all past bad happenings in a spice grinder
& start anew
lead me to the meat cleaver
if that is what is required.

someone needs to take the blame

i   .

if I had been a cutter   I would've done it   bled out   my guilt
from thin slits   on my forearm   & thighs   razor nick   here
razor nick   there   one deep slash   would have been too quick
the flagellation over too soon   self-scorn   it wants a prolonged
slow-drip display   cut   bleed   weep   cut   bleed   weep

ii.

instead I hemorrhaged   hotdogs   hostess twinkies   ice cream
made a good glue   held it all together   while I stabbed a finger
down my throat   & gagged   cut off the life in my windpipe
so that I could eject   all the knives   beneath

once   over party chitchat   a guest declared that bulimia
was a selfish act   just so they can stay skinny!   I defer
it is about swallowing razor-sharp scalpels   & crusting stitches
gobbling up   shattered glass   & bloodied pillows   every crumb
& sliver   of the horrors you most surely caused   & then trying
with all your might   to become a volcano   erupting its pain
gobble   swallow   spew   gobble   swallow   spew.

magic 8 ball
(oracle at spencer's gifts)

is it true
my husband now prefers his nose in a book
than lips to my navel?
reply hazy   try again

when will he tell me
the house has become too heavy
& he must go?
cannot predict now

at night   we are two busted boards on a mattress
his back   to my back   the staircase of our spines
riddled with splinters   pushing up against each other
enraged by the roulette wheel at the bottom of the stairs

at times   we hate each other for this
but   we still love each other   right?
concentrate & ask again.

my purse

it is the black spleen of my day
engorged with constant lies
one tube lipstick
poppy
one blush
candy ribbon
one button   yellow
found on the floor of an ambulance
one hospital parking stub   blue
one medicine bottle   brown
marked *valium*
use in case of convulsive seizure
the rubber stopper   thumb-worn
cracked from overuse

hunchbacked off my hip
my purse-as-spleen
swings back & forth
swollen with credit
insurance
reminder cards
even a punch tab from the pet store
for every ten bags of lamb nuggets
I get a free bag
the clerk always asks
& would you like to donate to the animal shelter today?
of course
it is good karma

when the homeless man on the corner
begs for his ten

my hands fumble for the granola bar
at the bottom of my spleen
here
I don't have any cash
he looks at the bar
aghast
this all you got?

I struggle to hold it all in
this organ vised to my thigh
loaded with corpses
dragons
voices
choices
pens with no tops
bang against nickels & dimes
receipts from target
costco
the doctors
the therapist
that woman who says she can heal
through the touch of her hands

a jar of *xanax*
rattles around the side pocket
shouting through the seams
empty out
empty out
empty out.

in this ring…

each day is a delilah in pink tutu
balancing one-legged atop a frothy white horse
she wears sequins & stardust
an ogre's pronged horns

a cyclone   it brews in the sewer
rats are eating away at the moon
a birthday cake leaves a plate empty
drool at the end of a spoon

knuckles up   I say

the bully waits in the bushes
fistful of splenetic stones
gloom is a savvy gigolo
sucking at weary bones

yes   there will be dust storms in the aquarium
algae slicking the streets
don your suit of armor
viking helmet with griffon motif

knuckles up   dear children   knuckles up

may your gloves be raptor handled
victory spattered   bespangled
each day is a delilah in pink tutu
saboteur in mesh tights.

pearly whites

my father kept his children's baby teeth   in a broken-spined box   at the bottom of his sock
drawer   there were seven   children   he had a lot of teeth   strewn in with a mess
of coins   tie clips   & a silver throwing star   the kind used by ninjas   in b-movies
I did sneak   peek   into that drawer often   transfixed by my father's keeping   of tiny teeth
he was not   a toucher   did not hug   or kiss   did not make breezy chitchat   nor guffaw
with wide-mouthed   abandon   one could say   he was stern   heart   padlocked
key misplaced   yet   he kept our teeth

once a mother   I   too   became a tooth collector   each little nib of ivory that dropped out
of my toddlers' mouths   as if these tokens   would somehow preserve my children   forever
where my father felt a need   to hide the teeth   of his most tender emotions   I carried mine
one might argue   too close to the gaping gums   spilling the teeth   out onto my palm
in the worst of moments   fingering them around in little circles across my skin
putting them on my tongue   & tasting their rusted blood   I needed this   my children
were still here   still alive   I had their teeth to prove it   when I spit them back into my fist
& shook my wrist   tempting the perfect roll of dice   oh   how I lucky I felt.

out of the haze

that leaden shroud
bleak chapel fog
the dull drag of walking
in boots with steel heels

out of the haze
the sun will lick cheekbones
with halvah & honey

stars will find home again
in that space behind eyelids
filling it with luxuriant dreams

the graceful sway of birch trees
tulips with buttery leaves

out of the haze
even gravel will feel like ermine
under skipping bare feet

things will seem wonderful again
out of the haze.

doctor he

not as in he or she
but *he*   as in *qinge*
the chinese surname for *celebrate*

doctor celebrate
she carried her name
in gleaming teeth & wry chuckles
as she tapped needles into my feet
between each of my toes
a delighted cobbler repairing a broken boot

the needles around the belly
button hurt the most
but were meant to trigger
the flow of my qi
or vital force

doctor celebrate's office
was lined with antique drawers
spilling with envelopes
of dried mushrooms
barks & herbs
ginseng
dang gui
gingko biloba

tea was brewing
steaming serenity from the mouth
of a porcelain pot

an entire window was embroidered

with leggy stalks of aloe & bamboo
each leaf & limb
sucking at the glass & sunshine

when doctor celebrate tapped a needle
between my eyebrows
she said that I might see a flash
like andromeda on fire
but very brief
& I did
& it was.

from the well-meaning

mouth your blessings every day can be a challenge yourself with optimistic
thoughts that trigger anxiety can blunt the soul is sacred & precious herbs
are worth a try saffron anise curry favors when needed write in a journal
all your dreams before they go up in smoke each room with sweetgrass
& sage advice is to curl underneath a cozy blanket the house with fresh
lilacs & rose petal baths can be so healing stones might help
fluorite malachite tanzanite from the fertile hills & hills of pills for blue
mood rings that turn bright orange when feeling happy is just a word full of
steam some jasmine tea leaves can be read by a fortune teller tell no one tell
anyone who will listen this is important to eat lots of greens from jade &
violet from amethyst can cut through what's holding you down by your
pillow sprinkle holy water from lourdes only knows what is next time
you will be stronger than a roman soldier on.

optimism

as feelings go 'tis
the bon mot
the rosy sip

when at its tip
(doubt   full stop)
one yearns to stomp
the streets euphoric   bang pots
spin tops

the eyes   a mist
eager   moist
(doubt   one day   post
mortem.)

inhale as needed

the dust on a butterfly's back
rings on a fallen tree
the dragonfly
with its windowpane wings
the rabbit with its almond gloss eyes

hope   that uncertain promise
it comes to me most fully
when there are acorns at my feet
a V of swans   up high
clouds   pages & pages of them
as they flip & turn through the sky.

breadcrumbs

& so this is where they have led me
bent kneed beneath a shaman in green
the trees – my priests
they welcome my palms   my cheeks
lips laid to branches
sun-soaked beams
my veins of shock & thunder
melted to woodland butter

melted to woodland butter
my veins of shock & thunder
sun   soaked beams   lips laid to
branches   they welcome my palms
my cheeks
the trees! my priests!
bent-kneed beneath a shaman in green
this is where they have led me.

soothsayer – thoughts from the oak

my arms
they ache from all this weight
look at all the woe hung on my boughs
trinkets wrapped in ribbon, carved out of tin
heart shapes, feet, earlobes, lungs

they have turned me into a carnival
of their own catastrophes
mouths calling out to me
cure my loneliness   cure my warts
my chest   it hurts every time I see my mother

what am I to do with these palsied prayers
and whispered wishes
at times, I find their pleading pitiful
and then am ashamed
have I not whimpered

under the cover of darkness
stroking my own lucky totems
roots thumbing the chip of an elk horn
bark clinging to the just-landed-ladybug

I once held onto a feather
tight in my boughs for days
pleading with my maker
and its exploding galaxies above

please, please
let a nest be built
right here

but one that does not
ask   too much.

green

green
is a jejune sapling
cradling a bud in velvet-green gloves
love   a blossom unfolding   right into her hands

green
is the sky above
riddled with sizzling green sparks
& dark   dark clouds
whipped into a wild green mast

green
is the jejune sapling
as this monster gales at its crown & feet
green & gruesome   hurling salt   & sleet

green
is grace
the elegance that comes from innocence
quick-shattered
the jejune that heaves up her arms   bud within
to hurl through the storm using jejune limbs

up   up   through the sparks   & the dark
she raises her child in hallelujah wrists
here   little love   take a glimpse
there are stars beyond
the lashing green beast

this   at the least
I can promise.

Notes

'butternut' refers to being born with jaundice.
Jaundice is a yellowing of the skin and whites of eyes
that happens when the body does not process bilirubin
properly. This may be due to a problem in the liver. It is
also known as icterus.

'not periwinkle' refers to a rare, life-threatening heart
condition called Tetralogy of Fallot. Tetralogy of Fallot
is caused by a combination of four heart defects that
are present at birth: pulmonary valve stenosis, ventrical
septal defect, overriding aorta & right ventricular
hypertrophy. Tetralogy of Fallot is fatal unless repaired
via open-heart surgery.

'yellow' is an homage to the words used by artist Vincent
Van Gogh in his many letters to his dear friend Emile
Bernhardt in the year before his death, 1890.

'doctor number six (your child has epilepsy)' references
Joan of Arc (patron saint of France), Lewis Carroll
(English author) & Vincent Van Gogh (Dutch painter),
all of whom suffered from epilepsy. Epilepsy is a surge
of volcanic electrical activity in the brain, often causing
convulsive seizures and even death. The word 'epilepsy'
comes from the Latin word epilepsia meaning "to
take hold of, seize upon, attack." Hippocrates called it
the Sacred Disease. Ayurvedic literature, dating back
to 400 BC, refers to epilepsy as apasmara, "lack of
consciousness." Epilepsy has also been called the falling
sickness.

'gram negative rods' refers to pulmonary endocarditis, an extremely uncommon, and often fatal, bacteria that invades the heart valve.

'from the well-meaning' is meant to leapfrog from word to word, one phrase bleeding and hopscotching into the next.

'optimism' is written in anagram form, using letters solely from the title in the last word of each sentence.

'breadcrumbs' models a mirror poem in which the first stanza repeats, backwards, in the following stanza.

'soothsayer – thoughts from the oak' refers to the prayer trees that are customarily seen around the world. People decorate these trees with small metal charms, ribbons, coins and personal notes written on paper. In some countries, even meat and chocolate have been hung from sacred trees to bring good luck, prosperity, health and love.

Acknowledgments

Danez Smith, wherever you are, thank you for the harsh
critiques and quiet encouragement.
Without your guidance this would have never happened.
And thank you to my Poetry Project
partners in crime, via The Loft Literary Center/
Minneapolis, Minnesota: Amy Buechler, Mary Harrold,
Ronda Redmond, Annette Schiebout & Mike Trost.
It was a year I will never forget. Intense, thrilling,
excruciating. Also, thanks to the amazing poets who
wrote such wonderful blurbs for my manuscript: Chris
Martin, Kita Shantiris and Ronda Redmond. I can only
hope to be half as talented as you. And to my editor,
Alex Wylie, of the velvet gloves and across-the-pond
weightlifting, my gratitude could not be more sincere.
And to Todd Swift and Amira Ghanim of Black Spring
Press Group/UK, thank you thank you thank you. Last,
the profoundest love to my yellow, my blue and my
husband-first-reader, John.